RE-DISCOVER FLORIDA

BY HAMPTON DUNN

To Stephanie
With Warm Regards
Hampton Dunn

TREND HOUSE / Tampa, Florida

©Copyright—1969, Hampton Dunn

Cover Photograph
FORT PICKENS, PENSACOLA
(Florida State News Photo)

L. C. Card Catalog No. 73-97006
All Rights Reserved.
Printed in the United States of America

For Florida Book Catalog, write
Trend House
P.O. Box 2350
Tampa, Florida 33601

To

EDWIN B. BROWNING, SR.

of Madison, Florida,

my eighth grade teacher in

a country school in Citrus County

who inspired his students to

aspire.

H. D.

FOREWORD

A "CRACKER" LOOKS AT FLORIDA

I was born in Florida and have lived here all my life. (No, I did not make either the first or second voyages with Ponce de Leon . . . my explorations began a little later on). I love Florida, every cubic inch of it . . . every linear foot of its 8,462 miles of coast line . . . every square yard of its rolling hills, piney wood flatlands, soupy Everglades, its citrus-producing ridge . . . every quart of water in Florida's lakes, rivers, bayous and bays.

This state which has so much to offer today also has a tremendously interesting and colorful background. Why, Florida is the oldest state in the Union and our ancestors were well colonized when the Mayflower came along upcountry and those folks got all the publicity.

The stirring history of the Sunshine State is often overlooked, possibly because we have such a vibrant present and booming future we fail to take inventory of the significant events and of the brave and bold and even sometimes reckless personalities who carved a great state from a jungle-like terrain.

Florida's genuinely attractive attractions such as Silver Springs, Cypress Gardens, the Seaquarium . . . these and many more . . . are so engaging, Floridians and visitors alike overlook landmarks and historical sites that reveal the story of Florida in the making, Florida of the ancient days, of the pioneer days, of the territorial days and on down the line.

There's scarcely a city, town or village in the state that doesn't have a memento of the past, a link that helps us get the feel of our noble forebears and their experiences in building this province.

It is my real pleasure to travel Florida almost constantly. From mile to mile, it is an ever-changing panorama. Let's not rush through Florida, hitting only the Interstates and seeing only the huge cities or the lovely beaches. Let's pause by the side of the road and look at this ante-bellum home, or that solid old fort, or this novel structure or that one. Let's slow down and gaze at the 18 or more primary lighthouses that have guarded our shores for lo, these many years. Let's meet and know some great Floridians, Dr. John Gorrie, who invented the ice-making machine and gave us air-conditioning; Henry M. Flagler, the multi-millionaire who truly was our greatest developer; let's know better one of the nation's presidents, Old Hickory Andrew Jackson, who was our own first Governor . . . Yes, we have a story to tell, a story with all the absorbing elements of an exciting TV serial or movie: drama, war, economic triumphs and setbacks, agricultural accomplishments.

"Re-Discover Florida" only scratches the surface of what Florida is all about. But we trust readers will develop a curiosity about us and will themselves then explore and "Re-Discover Florida."

HAMPTON DUNN
Tampa, Florida

Florida East Coast

HISTORY IS LOST ON OLD FORT AT NEW SMYRNA

NEW SMYRNA BEACH—They're standing there today, just as they have for possibly centuries, but their origin and history remain unknown. "They" are the foundations of an old fort that overlook the riverfront here just across from the yacht basin.

Believed to be an old Spanish fort, the landmark was discovered back in 1854 when an Indian mound was excavated. The relic is in good shape and makes an ideal play fort for youngsters of today, just as it probably has for many generations. The old fort is situated on Hillsborough Street between Washington and Julian streets.

New Smyrna's roots in history lie deep. It is said to have been occupied by Don Pedro Menendez de Aviles in 1565, after which his group deserted the spot and headed up the coast to St. Augustine.

The first developer was Dr. Andrew Turnbull who obtained a grant for 60,000 acres under the English Occupation Act in 1767. He brought over a colony of 1,500 persons of many nationalities. Included were Scotch, Syrians, Minorcans, Spanish, Moorish, Greek and others.

Turnbull's dreams of a prosperous sugar and indigo plantation did not pan out. By the time of the Revolution, he was ready to give up. The pioneers were permitted to leave New Smyrna if they wished. The majority went to St. Augustine.

8

FLORIDA'S HAVEN FOR SHIPWRECKED SAILORS

STUART—Gilbert's Bar House of Refuge on Hutchinson Island near here is the last of a group of lifesaving stations built in 1875 to aid shipwrecked sailors. Today it houses a marine laboratory, a museum of nautical and marine history and a sea turtle hatchery.

The rugged structure was erected by the U.S. Life Saving Service and was one of five such shelters built along the Florida east coast to take in shipwrecked sailors who made their way to shore.

The first keeper was Fred Whitehead of Saint Lucie who was appointed December 1, 1876, and was paid $40.00 a month. The salary later was raised to $500 a year.

The logbook of the House of Refuge reveals many thrilling stories of dramatic sea rescues. One of the first major rescues came on April 19, 1886, when the brigatine J. H. Lane, of Seasport, Maine, with eight crew members and a $13,640 cargo of molasses, headed for Cuba, was wrecked on a reef three-fourths of a mile from shore. The keeper and his assistants managed to haul the crew to the beach. It was stormy with a gale of wind blowing.

The log noted: "Cold wet, some hardly able to stand on their feet, it seemed hardly possible that they would be able to reach the station seven and a half miles distant, and the nearest shelter from the rain, that at intervals would pour down upon the already chilled and half dead men." But the keeper had a flask of brandy and gave the sailors a swig. Finally, all were safely inside the comfortable House.

9

WHEN MIAMI LIGHTHOUSE WAS A BLAZING CHIMNEY

MIAMI—In South Florida, where there were few white settlers, the Indians had the upper hand during the savage Seminole Wars. In mid-1836, the settlers fled to populated Key West for protection while the red men were on the warpath.

At Cape Florida on Key Biscayne here, even the lighthouse keeper had deserted his post because he was allergic to Indians. Not so, his brave and devoted assistant, John W. B. Thompson, who decided to stay at his post, come what may. A Negro helper, Henry, also elected to stand by.

At 4 P.M. on that hot July 23, 1836, the rampaging Indians struck. Thompson and Henry scooted inside the structure. They fired from the windows and staved off the attackers until dark. The Indians broke open the door and set fire to the stairway. Oil drums caught fire. The guards made their way to the top. In a final desperate attempt to halt the Indians, Thompson heaved over a box of ammunition below. It exploded and set off a furious blast, turning the lighthouse into a blazing cannon. The Negro helper was killed during the fracas. Thompson was rescued a day later by sailors from the U.S. schooner, Motto.

The Cape Florida lighthouse is the oldest structure in South Florida. After that disastrous day in 1836, the government rebuilt Cape Florida in 1837. The lenses and illumination equipment were destroyed by pirates in 1861. Cape Florida was dis-established in 1878. Today it is a new State Park.

KEYS' LIGHTHOUSES
WRECKED THE 'WRECKERS'

KEY WEST—Back before Florida became a state in 1821 the principal business in the Florida Keys was said to be wrecking.

The reefs along the keys were treacherous, and there were few navigation aids for the ship captains. Often they were wrecked. Local islanders made a career of helping to salvage the contents of the ships. For this they demanded, and got, a huge percentage of the cargo. It is even recorded that some unscrupulous wreckers would put out false beacons to lure ships to the reefs—instead of away from them.

Thus were the conditions when Uncle Sam stepped in and expanded his lighthouse system to the keys. The tale is handed down that many Key Westers opposed installation of the lights because it spelled the end for their highly prosperous wrecking business. In 1825 alone, $293,353 worth of wrecked property was sold in Key West. From 1831 to 1846 the proceeds from 50 wrecks stranded in the Florida Keys totalled more than a million dollars.

The first lighthouse in Key West was erected in 1825, survived several storms and eventually was destroyed. Others succeeded it including one built in 1840 and destroyed by the hurricane of 1846.

A modern lighthouse was built at a cost of $25,000. The one in Key West sits within the city limits. The light is 91 feet above water, has a candlepower of 50,000 and is visible nine miles at sea. It's the farthest inland of any in the country.

SHERMAN SERVED AT FORT DALLAS AS LIEUTENANT

MIAMI—This capital of Florida's Gold Coast hasn't always been the glittering, swinging place it is today. A little more than a century ago it was hardly big enough to call a village. (As late as 1920 its population was only 29,000!).

Development of this magic metropolis dates back to the days of the Seminole Wars when the Federal Government established Fort Dallas in what was then a wilderness but today is downtown Miami —and the site of the Dallas Park Hotel.

The U.S. Army was fighting the pesky Indian guerillas in a war similar to the modern day Vietnam battles, very costly in money and lives. Thus a string of forts was built. Fort Dallas was erected in 1836 about the time Dade County was created from Monroe County. The new county, effective Feb. 4, 1836, was named in honor of Maj. Francis L. Dade, current hero of the nation who was killed at Bushnell by Indians who wiped out Dade's whole company. (Dade had been stationed at the new fort in Miami shortly before his death).

Near the end of the war, a dashing Second Lieutenant, William Tecumseh Sherman, later to gain fame in the Civil War, was stationed at Fort Dallas, his first assignment after West Point graduation.

The stone barracks of Fort Dallas were moved, stone by stone, in 1924, from the original site to Lummus Park at Northwest Third Ave. and Fourth St. The old site had been sold to become a hotel site. Fort Dallas was abandoned in 1858 when all military posts in Florida were closed.

ARCHITECT CONVERTED ROAD
INTO RETREAT FOR PEDESTRIANS

MIAMI BEACH—Fashionable Lincoln Road, long a mecca for shoppers of America, is even more attractive since its conversion to a pedestrian mall.

Automobiles were outlawed on the street and the place became a veritable garden to lure foot traffic into the exclusive shops.

The man chosen to design this radical beautification and revitalization program for the shopping heart of the resort city was a hometowner, controversial Morris Lapidus.

A native of Russia, Lapidus came to America as an infant and studied architecture at Columbia. He's noted as the designer of the Fontainebleau, Eden Roc and Americana hotels here. Lapidus has been characterized as a man who blends "a deep insecurity and flashes of real arrogance with a fanatical devotion to the drawing board."

Be that as it may, he carried out well his aim to make Lincoln Road Mall so attractive that visitors would be irresistably drawn there as to other major tourist attractions. The designer felt four factors were necessary in creating an ideal shopping area: (1) Accessibility; (2) Large parking area; (3) Diversification and quantity of shops; and (4) Absence of traffic.

So it was he provided an abundance of tropical gardens, pools and fountains, shelters and many other unusual and esthetically appealing features. The Road merchants enthusiastically accepted his ideas and even voted assessments totaling $600,000 to finance the undertaking in 1960.

SPANISH KING GAVE AMERICAN
A PIECE OF FLORIDA

FORT GEORGE ISLAND—Don Juan McQueen had a lust for land. A Philadelphian by birth, he became prominent during the Revolutionary War through his friendship with big names like Washington and Jefferson and Lafayette.

McQueen started buying vast property in South Carolina and Georgia, finally became "land poor" and his creditors took back their land and chased McQueen down to Spanish-owned Florida. There he cuddled up to the administration, which desired friendly contacts with American big-wigs. So it was in 1791 that the King of Spain bestowed on McQueen Fort George Island at the mouth of St. Johns River. His Majesty also gave the American the fancy title of "Captain of Militia and Commandant of the St. Johns and St. Marys."

The new Floridian built some tabby houses on the island, and his own residence, which later became the property of another colorful figure, Zephaniah Kingsley, who housed his African princess in the McQueen House.

McQueen's family remained in Georgia and he was lonely on the island. Besides that his agricultural pursuits were failures due to bad weather. Finally, in 1804, McQueen sold the island and another large plantation at Ortega to John Houston McIntosh for $28,000.

The McQueen house, built of tabby brick and with a second story of wood, is regarded as the oldest habitable house in Duval County today, according to Dena Snodgrass of Jacksonville Historical Society.

U.S. 'GIBRALTAR' OBSOLETE BEFORE COMPLETION

KEY WEST—During the Civil War, this island community remained loyal to the U.S. and was the only Union stronghold in the South. The Yankees assumed control of Fort Taylor here and promptly proceeded to build four other fortresses to add protection.

Fort Taylor guarded the entrance to Key West Harbor and the other forts, including East Martello Tower, were begun during the war years. These auxiliary forts were designed to protect the big Fort from possible rear attacks. East and West Towers, each massive brick structures, were identical in plan. Although Key West labor plus 150 imported Irishmen worked furiously on the projects, neither fort was completed. Alas, all masonry forts were made obsolete early in the conflict by the development of the rifled naval gun and the explosive warhead! (A masonry fort near Savannah, Fort Pulaski, was wiped out by a Union naval force. Key West was never subjected to a naval attack.)

The name Martello seems to be a corruption of Martella Point on the island of Corsica where a fort of this type successfully resisted a British invading force in 1541. The term Martello Towers thus is used to designate masonry forts usually on seacoasts and which generally have thick walls and entrances high off the ground.

The Key West forts had various uses during the Spanish-American War and World Wars One and Two. Through the years, some of the brick have dissapeared and Key Westers used the forts as free brickyards for 90 years or more. The East Tower now is a museum and art gallery.

15

PRE-SPACE AGE RAILROAD
SERVED THE PLANETS

JUPITER—A bit south of the modern day moonport at Cape Kennedy lies this community which many years ago was a terminal for the so-called Celestial Railroad. It was so-called because the line served the heavenly bodies of Jupiter, Neptune, Mars, Venus and Juno.

Formally named the Jupiter and Lake Worth Railway, it soon got its nickname. It operated between 1889 and 1895 and hauled freight and passengers from this town to the Lake.

The train usually consisted of a cabbage-head engine whose engineer reportedly could toot out "Dixie" on the whistle, and a passenger car and several freight cars. It took a half-hour to run between the two points, if it ran on schedule. Sometimes the crew and passengers liked to stop and hunt along the way.

Back in those days, Juno was the county seat of Dade County. In the early 1890s, the great Florida developer Henry M. Flagler busily extended his railroad down the East Coast. During construction, he was forced to use the Celestial Railroad to haul materials. This was costly. Flagler got revenge, by-passing the Jupiter-Juno peninsula. In 1889 it is alleged that the county records were stolen and the county seat was removed to Miami. The Celestial Railroad had gone out of business.

The Seminole Chapter of the Daughters of American Revolution has erected a Monument to the Celestial Railroad commemorating the eight-mile, narrow-gauge road.

THE CITY HALL THAT DOESN'T LOOK LIKE ONE

CORAL GABLES—For more than 40 years, proud residents of this beautiful city have boasted of their unique City Hall. And well they might. It doesn't look like the kind of city hall you fight. You just brag about its fine architecture that blends in so perfectly with the rest of the community.

It's a top example of the renowned Mediterranean style of architecture which prevails throughout this boom-time neighborhood. As a matter of fact, it is a replica of the municipal building in Seville.

Strange as it may seem, George Merrick, the founder of the Gables, never traveled abroad, but he admired Spanish, Italian, Venetian, Moorish and Tunisian styles of designing and chose them for Coral Gables, starting with City Hall which embodied elements of all the types.

The municipal structure anchors the street known as the Miracle Mile, home of a fabulous shopping area. A dominating feature of City Hall is the campanile, or bell tower, and bronze belfry copied from Seville's building. The tall columns in front reflect the Venetian influence and the rounded front is Italian in nature.

Native stone is used throughout the building. The tiles on the roof were obtained in Spain and Cuba in exchange for U.S.-made roofing materials!

The unusual City Hall is part of the grand dream Merrick had for his modern city, a dream which came true—and then some.

AN ANCIENT CIVIL DEFENSE SHELTER

ST. AUGUSTINE—One of the earliest and the longest-lasting "air raid" shelters in America is the ancient Castillo de San Marcos here.

One of the purposes for erecting the mighty fortress in the late 1700s was to protect the population of this pioneer city. The sprawling structure with thick masonry walls was designed as a shelter in an emergency. Indeed, it has been a haven for as many as 1,500 persons during a siege.

The Spanish who founded St. Augustine tried to protect the town from enemy attack, the English traders, pirates, Indians and others who were menacing to the Spanish treasure fleets. No less than eight wooden forts had fallen, one by one, including a structure destroyed by Sir Francis Drake, before the stone fort was started.

Construction began in 1672 and continued for 24 years. It was built of native coquina rock, basically hardened sea shells. The fort is a symmetrical structure, with four bastions, a perfection of Italo-Spanish engineers. The gigantic walls are from 9 to 16 feet thick and 30 feet high, and the fortress is surrounded by a moat. Indian slave labor was used to build the fortress, which is the oldest masonry military structure in the United States. The fort was put to the test in 1740 when James Oglethorpe of Georgia beseiged the Castillo for 38 days without success. When Florida became a state, the fort was renamed Fort Marion honoring Revolutionary War hero Gen. Francis Marion, but later reverted to its original name.

'THE WEATHER IS BALMY AND SO IS FISHER'

MIAMI BEACH—An unusual monument to an unusual person at Alton Road and 50th St. features the figure of a kindly man with a slouch hat. It's a salute to Carl Graham Fisher and also carries the legend: "He Carved a Great City From a Jungle."

And so he did. Like a hero in a Western movie, he came dashing forward in 1915 with his fortune and rescued John S. Collins and the Lummus brothers, J.N. and J.E., who had run out of money in trying to develop the beach. Fisher, who'd gotten rich selling Prest-O-Lite gas auto lights and at one time was owner of the Indianapolis Speedway, loaned the pioneers $200,000. But that was just the beginning of his investment in this tropical isle. He spent six million before selling the first lot and eventually poured $50 million in the development.

He was a real promoter. He brought in a pair of Indian elephants Rosie and Carl, to help clear the "jungle"; offered waterfront lots free to any one who would build. He offered the oceanfront property where the Roney Plaza later was located to any one who'd build a $150,000 hotel on it. There were no immediate takers.

The Fishers built their own home, "The Shadows" on the ocean at Lincoln Road. It later became a gambling place. He built the first luxury hotel, The Flamingo. Although he was flamboyant in his promotion of Miami Beach what he really had in mind was a community similar to Palm Beach. He built polo fields and promoted other sports.

Fabulous Miami Beach itself is a monument to Carl Fisher and a rebuke to those who chided: "the weather is balmy and so is Fisher."

KEY WEST INSPIRED
FAMED PAINTER OF BIRDS

KEY WEST—John James Audubon was a restless soul who liked to roam and to paint native birds in their natural habitats. This search to paint brought him to the then "wild" town of Key West, the latter part of 1831 and early part of 1832 to pursue his life's work.

In a pleasant second-story room of the home of Capt. John H. Geiger, a sea captain and master salvager, sometimes called "wrecker," Audubon sketched the birds of the Florida Keys. These went into his brilliant collection, "Birds of North America." Looking out the window of the Geiger home, he painted the white-crowned pigeon. He also painted the Key West quail-dove which he named in appreciation of Key West's hospitality to him.

These paintings were reproduced in the famous Elephant Folio, so called because of their size. These were some of the largest books ever printed, 30 by 40 inches. One complete four-volume set is on display now at the Audubon House, a museum at present.

The historic home was snatched from destruction by Mitchell Wolfson, a Key West native who became a successful Miami Beach businessman, a few years ago. Doomed to make way for a parking lot, the house was saved by Wolfson's foundation and restored to its former splendor. The Sheraton, Regency and Empire pieces that are now in the house are much like those that might have been salvaged from ships wrecked off the Florida reefs in the 1800s. That, by the way, was how Geiger obtained the original furnishings.

MIAMI'S SALUTE TO GOOD NEIGHBORS TO SOUTH

MIAMI—This city is the gateway to Latin America and has strong ties with our neighbors to the South.

The people here wanted to create a tangible sign of good will and lasting friendship to let the world know its warm feeling for Pan America. So it was the attractive Torch of Friendship monument was erected at one of the most conspicuous spots in Miami—in Bayfront Park alongside busy Biscayne Boulevard.

Feature of the layout is a torch with a perpetual flame, atop an 18-foot obelisk. Natural gas provides fuel for the flame which burns continuously.

The city's warm expression of hope and peace is enhanced with the back-grounding eight-foot-high, 40-foot long curved stone wall. Imbedded in this are the seals of each of the American republics. Native stone quarried from the Florida Keys was used in the construction of both the shaft and the wall.

The Torch of Friendship was erected in 1960. After the assassination of President John F. Kennedy in 1963, the monument was dedicated to the memory of the late President.

THE GREATEST JIGSAW PUZZLE OF THEM ALL

NORTH MIAMI—Noted publisher William Randolph Hearst searched the world over in his prowl for art treasures. In 1925, he discovered and purchased a long-forgotten Spanish Monastery which in 1835 had been confiscated by the Spanish Government and sold to a farmer to store grain.

Today, the Monastery is erected in North Miami just off U.S. 1 and attracts people of all faiths. It is the oldest structure in the Western Hemisphere, predating Columbus' discovery of the New World by 351 years.

In the 12th Century, Alphonso VII, King of Leon, Castile and Galicia drove away the Moors from his kingdom. In gratitude to God, he founded in 1141 the Monasterio de San Bernardo de Sacramenia. It was operated by the Cistercian Order for 694 years.

Hearst had intended to transport the architectural gem to his estate in San Simeon, California. The more than 36,000 heavy pieces were packed in some 10,751 crates and shipped to New York. There they were stored and not moved because of the depression. Finally, two Ohio businessmen bought the Monastery and re-assembled it in sunny Florida. To put together the enormous jigsaw took 19 months and cost $1.5 million.

It is situated in a quiet, formal Spanish garden and the Monastery contains priceless treasures from the art, warfare and religious life of long-dead Middle Ages.

The Monastery is now owned by the St. Bernard Foundation, a non-profit corporation. It is used for Episcopal services on Sunday.

"IT IS NOT ANYBODY'S DAMN BUSINESS . . ."

FT. GEORGE ISLAND—A distinctive personality in Florida history was Zephaniah Kingsley, a native Scotsman who came to this country as a boy and migrated to Laurel Grove, Fla., in 1803.

The well-educated Kingsley was a coffee buyer at one time but was best known as a shrewd slave trader. He fell in love and married Anna Madgigene Jai, daughter of a chief of Senegal, on the east coast of Africa. His father-in-law assisted him in procuring slaves.

Kingsley moved to Florida, then under the Spanish flag because he foresaw the U.S. would outlaw the importation of slaves. This happened in 1807. The slave trader acquired Ft. George Island, near the mouth of St. Johns River, in 1817. He paid only $7,000 for it, a bargain even then.

Several houses used by the family still stand and are part of a State Park here. Kingsley believed in taking good care of his slaves and in training them well. They always brought premium prices on the market because of their skill.

Kingsley was described by a high official as a "classical scholar" and he was appointed by the U.S. President to the second Legislative Council. Kingsley's niece was Anna Matilda NcNeill Whistler, the "Mother" in the famous painting by her son, James Whistler.

Mrs. Whistler was one of the heirs, who challenged the will of Kingsley who left his property to his African wife noting "It is not anybody's damn business what I do with it . . ."

23

JACKSONVILLE'S "TREATY OAK" IS 300 YEARS OLD

JACKSONVILLE—The historic "Treaty Oak" is located near downtown Jacksonville. It is more than 300 years old, and, under its giant branches, several important treaties with the Indians were made.

The sprawling tree is a symbol of the colorful history of this city on the St. Johns River, one of the earliest in the state. The French Huguenots pioneered this area in 1562 and subsequently were chased away by the Spanish under Pedro Menendez.

This city arose from a ford in the river where Indians used to cross their cattle. They called it Wacca Pilatka, the Indian language for "cows crossing over." As time went by, it was referred to as Cow Ford, although the Spaniards called it the Ferry of St. Nicholas. Cow Ford it continued to be called until Florida became a territory in 1821. In 1822, Jacksonville was platted and named in honor of Andrew Jackson, the first territorial governor.

Jacksonville was first incorporated in 1832. It has had a stormy life since, figuring prominently in the Indian Wars, the Civil War and the Spanish American War as well as more recent conflicts.

In 1901, tragedy struck the city of 28,429, as a raging fire reduced Jacksonville to shambles. From the charred ruins, the courageous citizens set about rebuilding and developed one of the South's metropolitan areas. Annexation in 1969 took in most of Duval County, making Jacksonville the largest city, landwise, in the free world!

VIRGINIA DARE NOT FIRST WHITE YOUNGUN BORN IN U.S.!

JACKSONVILLE—The Fort Caroline National Memorial near here marks the site of the first European colony on the North American continent this side of Mexico. It represents France's bold bid to get into the great competition for New World territory.

The French hero who touched down here on May Day, 1562, was Huguenot Jean Ribault. He called what is now St. Johns River, the River of May. He presented the friendly Timucuan Indians a column in honor of King Charles IX. He then went on to South Carolina, where he left a small garrison and returned home.

Ribault's mariner on that trip, Rene de Laudonniere, headed up a new expedition of some 300 Huguenots who landed at the St. Johns site on June 25, 1564 and founded Fort Caroline.

Take it from present day Congressman Charles E. Bennett, a scholar and researcher into the history of the French exploits here, eight or ten white children were born at the fort. Since this was more than two decades before Virginia Dare saw the light of day in the Virginia colony, it disputes the historical legend that Virginia was the first white child born in this country. She was the first child born of English parents.

Ribault's folks had a rough time surviving in the new world, and the Spanish did not want them on Spanish land. An armada led by Pedro Menendez de Aviles sailed under orders from King Philip to wipe out the French and to get a foothold for the Spanish in Florida. He did both, establishing St. Augustine on Sept. 8, 1565, and smashing Fort Caroline a few days later.

25

THE CHURCH
HARRIET BEECHER STOWE BUILT

MANDARIN—The howling winds of Hurricane Dora in September, 1963 wiped out historic Episcopal Church of Our Saviour in this charming, moss-draped community. This is the church that famed Civil War writer Harriet Beecher Stowe helped to found and build.

Mrs. Stowe and her husband, the Rev. Calvin Stowe, a Presbyterian minister, moved here in 1867. The author of the controversial "Uncle Tom's Cabin" planned to do philanthropy among the Negroes. The Stowes started religious work in the community.

In 1881, an Episcopal clergyman, the Rev. Charles M. Sturgess, came here and started a mission for his denomination. Mrs. Stowe was a recent convert to the Episcopal Church. By Easter the following year, the building fund for a church structure totaled $500. Mrs. Stowe created the Mandarin Amateur Dramatic Association to put on plays for the benefit of the building fund. In 1883 the Church was raised on a high bluff overlooking the St. Johns River at a cost of $250. It was a copy of a mountain chapel in upstate New York. This was the last winter the Stowes stayed in Florida. The Rev. Mr. Stowe died in 1886.

The noted writer asked that the end window be reserved for a stained glass memorial for her husband. It was not until 1916, long after Mrs. Stowe's death in 1896, that a Tiffany window was installed. It depicted a great live oak, "symbol of the Stowes' love of Mandarin."

The vicious hurricane ripped through Mandarin and smashed the building—including the Stowe memorial window. A new church with a chapel duplicating the old one was dedicated in 1966.

26

TRAGEDY STRUCK PRESIDENT'S KIN IN PIONEER FLORIDA

ENTERPRISE—Almost at the back stoop of a private dwelling here is the grave of Polly Taylor, said to be the first white person buried south of St. Augustine.

On the marble slab marking the tree-shaded burial site is inscribed: "Sacred to the memory of our beloved Polly, daughter of C. and C. Taylor, who departed this life of typhus fever September 21, 1842, age 13 years and 13 days. Major C. Taylor was the first settler at Enterprise, Florida, in 1841 when the country was full of Seminole Indians, and in the midst of their nation there was no white settlement nearer than St. Augustine and left in 1847."

A native Virginian, Maj. Cornelius Taylor was a first cousin of President Zachary Taylor, who as a General was one of the famous Indian fighters of pioneer Florida. Major Taylor moved from St. Augustine in 1841 to this quiet community on Lake Monroe, bringing with him his wife, little Polly and nine Negro slaves. He operated a sawmill here and was the first man to operate a steam power boat on the St. Johns River.

About a year after settling here, an epidemic of typhus fever broke out. A victim was Polly, whose real name was Arabella, the teenage daughter of the Major. Her grave is at the original Taylor residence, which was called Bueno Retiro.

According to local historian, Judge Robert H. Wingfield, the pioneer Major Taylor never fully recovered from t h e shock of Polly's death. He became restless and decided to move to California, in 1847. He stayed in Texas for a few years enroute to the coast. From Texas he put out to sea on a steamer which was caught in a Gulf hurricane and went down. Major Taylor was lost at sea.

27

"REMEMBER THE 'MAINE,' TO HELL WITH SPAIN!"

KEY WEST—The people who lived in this remote Florida Keys capital had a front row seat for the brief but violent Spanish-American War near the turn of the century. And there are many memories of that conflict existing here today.

The final straw that broke relations between the U.S. and Spain during the Cuban struggle for independence was the sinking of the battleship, "The USS Maine." She was blown up in Havana harbor on Feb. 15, 1898. Spain sought arbitration over responsibility but the American public, inflamed by a noisy metropolitan press, called for war. It is said that William Randolph Hearst's coverage of the Maine sinking "still stands as the orgasmic acme of truthless newspaper jingoism."

The Maine and her crew had spent much time in Key West. Townsfolk gave them a big party the night before they sailed for Fort Jefferson and Havana. The shocking news of her sinking reached here by motor launch, and Key West became the news center of the nation as reporters flocked here to get near the war action. About 50 of the Maine sailors were rushed to the city hospital where they died. They're buried in an enclosed area of the Key West Cemetery. A monument of a sailor was erected by local citizens to honor the lads. Yearly services are held in their memory. One of the turrets from the Maine is displayed at the corner of Southard and Margaret streets.

'PAPA' HEMINGWAY WROTE HIS BEST IN KEY WEST

KEY WEST—In a Spanish Colonial mansion which met his requirements—"big, comfortable and cool"—Ernest Hemingway produced some of his best novels as a resident of this isolated community, the southernmost in the United States.

The Hemingway House, at 907 Whitehead St., across the street from the historic Key West Lighthouse, now is a museum and shrine to the famed writer who owned it from 1931 until his death in 1961. Mr. and Mrs. Jack Daniel bought it for $80,000, tried living there for a couple of years, were overrun by Hemingway fans, then finally gave up and turned the home into a museum.

Among the works "Papa" completed in this tropical setting were "For Whom the Bells Toll," "A Farewell to Arms," "Green Hills of Africa," "To Have and To Have Not" (with its background of Key West), "The Snows of Kilimanjaro," "The Fifth Column" and "The Macomber Affair."

The structure dates back to 1851, built by Asa Tift, a Key West businessman. Hemingway turned the Carriage House i n t o a Pool House and studio where he wrote. The Nobel prize winner had the first swimming pool built in Key West. It was so costly, he tossed a one-cent coin into the wet cement and remarked that the pool had taken his last penny.

The mansion contains furniture, rugs and mementos collected by Hemingway from various parts of the world, especially Spain. Exotic trees and plants flourish on the grounds. Hemingway used to drive up the Florida Keys and dig many of the plants now thriving at the house.

29

A FORT WAS BUILT
AROUND THE LIGHTHOUSE

GARDEN KEY—Way out here in the Dry Tortugas isles, some 69 miles west of Key West in the Gulf of Mexico, is a lighthouse that has been in operation since 1825. It pre-dates the massive Fort Jefferson surrounding it by 20 years.

For years this cluster of coral islets was the hangout for pirates. When the U.S. took over Florida in 1821, the buccaneers were chased away. Then, for additional insurance to a growing United States commerce in the Gulf, a lighthouse was built on Garden Key. Thirty-one years later the present 150-foot light was erected on nearby Loggerhead Key.

The contract for lights at Cape Florida, Dry Tortugas and Sambo Key was let to Samuel B. Lincoln of Hingham, Mass., in July, 1824. Shortly after that he was lost at sea on a trip to the Keys and his bondsmen were directed to pick up the contract. It was constructed and Keeper William Flaherty and his wife arrived in late 1825.

A spokesman for the U.S. Coast Guard reports that Flaherty's "industry and enthusiasm left something to be desired. He failed to keep his wicks trimmed and the lantern panes were so black no light showed through." It also developed that, "Mrs. Flaherty was unhappy, fresh provisions didn't arrive often enough and social life was nil. Travel opportunities were restricted and mosquitos terrible." She wrote a letter to President Adams' wife complaining. Flaherty was transferred shortly. When Fort Jefferson was built around the lighthouse, this quarter of an acre remained lighthouse property.

UNUSUAL MONUMENT SYMBOLIZES FRIENDSHIP

CORAL GABLES—One of the most unusual monuments is found here on Cartagena Plaza, where LeJeune, Sunset and Old Cutler Roads meet. The center of interest in a beautifully landscaped traffic circle is the monument featuring a pair of old shoes.

The shoes, "Los Zapatos Viejos," are replicas on a reduced scale of a famed statue in Cartagena, Columbia, in South America. That community is a Sister City of Coral Gables in the People to People program. The giant shoes on a stone base remind of the friendly ties between the two cities. The program between Coral Gables and Cartagena has won the Reader's Digest Foundation "best in the nation" award.

A plaque at Cartagena Plaza explains why the old shoes. It seems that a well-known Columbian poet, Luis Carlos Lopez, compared his feelings for his native city, Cartagena, to the affection that one has for a pair of comfortable old shoes, in his poem, "A Mi Ciudad Nativa." It's a quaint but effective manner of expressing fondness for home.

Friendly ties with Spanish neighbors on the South come naturally for Coral Gables which has Spanish atmosphere throughout. It is the beautifully planned city of George E. Merrick, which blossomed out during the Florida boom. The developer and his wife got names for most of the streets from Washington Irving's book, The Alhambra.

The leading spokesman for the new city was the brilliant orator William Jennings Bryan, who was paid $50,000 a year to extol its virtues.

31

WHITEHALL, THE TAJ MAHAL OF NORTH AMERICA

PALM BEACH—An aging Henry Morrison Flagler ordered his architects to "Build me the finest home you can think of" as a bridal gift to his third wife, a lady half his age. But later while living in the elegant Whitehall, Flagler confided to a friend, "I wish I could swap it for a little shack."

The multi-multi-millionaire railroad and hotel tycoon, who is probably Florida's greatest developer of all times, had this fabulous dream palace built for Mary Lily Kenan, a pretty North Carolina belle who loved fun and to give parties for their socialite friends. The couple was wed in August, 1901, after Flagler had obtained a divorce from his second wife on grounds of insanity. The architect Carrere and Hastings got busy right away, designed the splendid mansion, furnished it with prized possessions from across the world and it was ready to move in by 1902. It had cost two and a half million to build, another million and a half to furnish.

A reporter of the day noted "Pilgrims with poetic fancy will find in Whitehall beauties that are grouped nowhere else on earth. To go from room to room is to go from century to century." The home immediately was titled, "The Taj Mahal of North America."

Flagler died here in 1913. He had fallen on a marble step and became feeble. His death at 83 was attributed to old age and exhaustion. The young Mrs. Flagler survived him only to 1917, continuing to live in Whitehall. Eventually the estate became a swank hotel, but a granddaughter of Flagler's recovered it in 1959 and opened it as a museum.

32

SUGAR MILL OR MISSION RUINS, IT'S INTERESTING

NEW SMYRNA BEACH—A mile or so off U.S. 1 here is an interesting stone structure preserved by the State as a historic memorial.

Sometimes it is referred to as the ruins of the "Mission of Atocuimi." It is said to have been built by the Spaniards in the 1600s for the Jororo Indians. The mission was burned a few years later and when the British came along it was used as a sugar mill. In the 1830s a sugar mill was started here for the Depeyster and Cruger firm. The Indians put the torch to it during their war with the white man.

A brochure issued by the State Parks explains: "Mrs. Jeannette Thurber Connor and her husband, Washington E. Connor, thoughtfully and reverently purchased the site of the Cruger and Depeyster ruins in 1893 and deeded it to the Florida State Historical Society in 1928. They believed the ruins to be the remains of an old Spanish mission, converted into a sugar mill. This error is understandable as the well-formed arches could well grace a church, a chapel or a mission."

Part of the history of the mission is that in 1696 the Indians rebelled against an order of Fray Luis Sanchez, a priest, who forbade their observance of certain tribal customs. The priest and two of his Indian converts were slain and the church ornaments were stolen.

The sugar mill ruins which remain today are of native coquina rock. One of the iron kettles is still around and the "walking beam" of the engine remains.

DUKE WED BEER HEIRESS, BUILT A 'CASTLE'

TITUSVILLE—A truly distinctive East Coast landmark is being preserved in a public park here, although it was displaced from its original setting on Merritt Island by the National Aeronautics and Space Administration.

It is the odd, octagonally-shaped "Duke's Castle," once the social center of the famed Dummitt Grove. History buffs in Brevard County had the cypress home moved when the property was taken over for the Spaceport expansion.

The Castle was built by Eicole Tamajo, Duke of Castlellucia, an Italian nobleman who had married Jennie Anheuser of the Budweiser beer family, after he acquired the pioneer grove in 1881. The couple entertained lavishly for awhile, but reportedly they did not live happily ever after. In fact, they had such a severe argument, they separated. The Duke went back to Italy. He died in 1892. The house meantime had been partitioned, one side for the nobleman and the other side for the American heiress.

Some of the material for the 22-room, two-story mansion came from the sailing ship Santa Cruz which had run aground near Daytona Beach. For instance, each of the two spiral stairways utilized ship masts for a center post. Planking on the outside is 30 feet long and 10 inches wide.

Most of the rooms, like the house itself, are octagonal in shape. The house design was adopted as a streamlining measure against gales and hurricanes.

The Dummitt Grove was planted by Douglas D. Dummitt in the early 1830's, using budwood from stock originally brought to Florida by the Spanish.

34

MATANZAS IS SPANISH FOR 'MASSACRE'

FORT MATANZAS NATIONAL MONUMENT—They call it Rattlesnake Island, this water-surrounded stone fort with the bloody name of Matanzas, which is Spanish for "massacre."

The weird name comes from that dreadful fortnight back in 1565 when the Spanish explorer Don Pedro Menendez, founder of St. Augustine, ordered the execution of several hundred French Huguenots to wipe out any French challenge to his nation's holdings in the New World. The fort stands in a waterway known as Matanzas Inlet.

Menendez was lauded by King Phillip II of Spain for the slaughter not because the victims were French, but because they were Lutherans which he regarded as "pirates." They had surrendered unconditionally.

Down through the years this little military outpost has figured in other historic events. After attacks by the British, by pirates and by Indians, the Spanish finally built the fort. It was completed in 1742 and looked then as it does today, a sturdy masonry structure with a minaret-like sentry box. It served through the years as a vital defense to St. Augustine. The stone was native coquina quarried from the King's quarry on nearby Anastasia Island.

The fort ruin was designated a National Monument by Presidential proclamation in 1924. It is 14 miles south of St. Augustine on Florida A1A. The Monument includes 308 acres on Rattlesnake Island, where the fort is located, and Anastasia Island, where the visitor center is. The fort is accessible only by boat.

35

'TRIUMPH IN RECALLING A GOLDEN AGE'

MIAMI—There could be no more appropriate or finer setting for the Dade County Art Museum than "Vizcaya," the Italian-style palazzo created by James Deering, the bachelor farm equipment magnate.

National Geographic magazine, a good judge of such things, describes Vizcaya as "a triumph in recalling a golden age of art and architecture . . . a repository of Italian decorative art, unexcelled in America."

When the International Harvester executive in 1914 started construction of a dream palace to house his marvelous collection of treasures from Europe, it caused a boomlet in the town of Miami (pop. then, 10,000). He employed more than 1,000 Miamians, plus hundreds of artisans from Europe.

In addition to the magnificent home, the 10-acre formal garden is also an attraction. And, as a breakwater, offshore from the steps leading to Biscayne Bay, there is a sculptured barge, a stone version of Cleopatra's.

Cost of the estate has been variously estimated from five millions to 15 millions. Whatever it was, Deering spared no expense. He wanted weathered tiles, so he sent agents to Cuba with instructions to buy the roofs of entire villages.

Vizcaya was opened on Christmas Day, 1916. Deering often entertained famous friends, but there were no "wild parties." Deering enjoyed living in his palace only 810 days. He died aboard ship while returning from Europe in 1925.

In 1952, Dade County bought Vizcaya for $1,000,000. It is now an art museum.

IT IS SLAVES' MARKET, NOT SLAVES MARKET

ST. AUGUSTINE—If you refer to the old shed in the Plaza area here as slaves market, be certain you put an apostrophe on it and call it "slaves' market" if you wish to be accurate.

Some tourists guide book writers have said that at one time slaves used to be auctioned off here. But you may take the word of one of the nation's foremost historians, Earle W. Newton, that the yarn about selling slaves here is just a myth.

Newton adds that it is quite possible that slaves themselves traded here. After all, it was a public market, first established by Spanish Gov. Mendez de Ganzo when he laid out the town plaza in 1597. He also set up the first standard system of weights and measures and enforced it. In the early days ships unloaded at the waterfront nearby. At this market, the folks bought their food staples, such as bread, flour, fish and meat and it was a busy place in the cool early morning. An early day supermarket, if you will.

In 1964, the late Dr. Martin Luther King chose St. Augustine as the site to make one of his first dramatic demonstrations for civil rights, and it is believed the so-called "slaves market" served for him as a symbol of mistreatment of Negroes in bygone years. Dr. King made many speeches at the Plaza during that "long, hot Summer."

The present public market building was originally constructed in 1824, shortly after the U.S. took over Florida, and was reconstructed after the 1887 fire.

37

CENTRAL FLORIDA

QUEEN OF ENGLAND GAVE GIFTS TO LAKELAND CHURCH

LAKELAND—The All Saints Episcopal Church, S. Massachusetts Ave. and E. Lemon St., is unique in having an old church enclosed within the present structure. The Chapel, located south of the High Altar, entered from the east end of the south aisle, is a replica of the original church. Its furnishings and plan are the same as the first little English church founded in Acton, then rural Lakeland, in 1884.

Acton was quite a pretentious village established between Lakes Bonney and Parker. Most of the population were natives of England, Scotland and Ireland, and was almost exclusively men. It was named for an English family whose head at the time was Lord Acton. It was an ill-advised venture and destined to a very short life, ending about 1889.

The new Floridians naturally wanted to build a church to worship as they had been taught by their fathers. The resident manager made a trip to England, put on lectures about "Florida" and charged admission fees all of which were used to finance construction of the first building.

The late Herbert J. Drane, distinguished Congressman for many years and long a historian for All Saints, recorded that "The Princess of Wales, afterwards the Queen of England (Alexandra, 1844-1925), (wife of Edward VII), became interested and gave to the little church certain altar furnishings, consisting . . . of some brass vases and perhaps some altar hangings, all of which disappeared very soon by the hands of vandals—the church being segregated and having no regular caretaker . . ."

An Episcopal congregation was formed in Lakeland in 1888 and this group moved the little Acton church building to town, using oxen for transport. The new and present edifice was built in 1924 and the old church was permanently recalled through design of the Chapel incorporated in the new structure.

"WAY DOWN UPON DE SWANEE RIBBER"

WHITE SPRINGS—Florida loves Stephen Collins Foster. He wrote what has been adopted as our State Song and made the Suwannee River one of the best known attractions in the state. But Foster himself never saw the Suwannee, nor Florida for that matter.

There is a splendid Stephen Foster Memorial at this point on the scenic river. White Springs is situated on U.S. 41 and only three miles off Interstate 75. A 200-foot carillon tower, which also houses the world's largest set (97) of tubular bells, is a focal point of the 243 acre park which was dedicated in 1950.

Foster was a native of Pittsburgh. Although his compositions were popular during his lifetime, he didn't profit much from them. His life's income was about $15,000. He died in a charity ward at New York's Bellevue at the age of 37 in 1864. In his purse after death were found three pennies, 35 cents in script and a piece of paper on which was written: "Dear Friends and Gentle Hearts." The title of another Foster hit? Probably.

There are several tales about how he selected the Suwannee River to immortalize in song. A kinsman claims he chose it from an atlas and changed the spelling from Suwannee to "Swanee." Another version is that he had picked "Way Down Upon the Pee Dee River" because it sounded musical, but the publisher changed it. At any rate his "Old Folks at Home," originally published under the name of famous minstrel Edwin P. Christy as composer (Foster sold his rights for $15), became a hit tune and in 1935 was adopted as Florida's State Song by the Legislature.

TIMUCUAN INDIANS, OF PRE-COLUMBUS DAYS, LEFT CLAN

GAINESVILLE—Way back yonder, Florida was occupied by the Indians. And for some time before Columbus discovered America, they were scattered in all sections of the state. From the Tampa Bay northward, the Timucuan Indians resided. They were a more docile people than their neighbors to the south, the Caloosas. The Timucuans offered very little resistance to the conquistadors .and, indeed, even welcomed missionaries as friends.

In the Florida State Museum in downtown Gainesville area are a couple of outstanding mementoes of the Timucuans. Near the entrance is the horned owl totem pole which was made by these tribes about 1350 A.D. It was found and dredged from the St. Johns River near DeLand by Victor Roepke in 1955.

The 10-foot figure was carved from a single piece of pine. It probably served as a symbol or totem for a village or a family group (clan).

It is explained at the Museum that there were many such poles in pre-Columbian times in the Southeastern U.S., but except for minor fragments, the only two known examples are the horned owl totem and the eagle totem, which also is on display here. The interesting eagle totem was donated to the Museum by N. F. Norton.

Indians in the Southeast U.S. also used other kinds of poles in connection with special ceremonies and ball games.

41

HISTORIC OLD DREW
MANSION ROTS AWAY

ELLAVILLE—Perched on the banks of the fabled Suwannee River near Ellaville, which is near Madison, is a ghostly mansion which was the former home of Gov. George Franklin Drew. He was the first governor to defeat the Carpetbaggers during Reconstruction.

Governor Drew was a well-to-do lumberman and he operated a sawmill on the west side of the Withlacoochee River just above its confluence with the Suwannee. While he was Governor (1877-81), he commuted by train to Tallahassee from his home.

There have been serious efforts to save the old homestead here. The State owned it for awhile and spent $10,000 trying to save it. The building was in bad shape and a survey showed that the structure was stripped of all fireplaces, windows and hardware. The old frame home was just a shell, the heavy timbers beneath it were rotten and several times the river flooded the house to a level of three feet above the first floor.

This old home stood in almost regal majesty and was the cultural center of North Florida.

The region's historian, Edwin B. Browning of Madison told newsmen recently that the old house has been fenced and posted, but it's just sitting there, rotting.

"A stranger passing there in a few years can say 'this too has gone with the wind,'" Browning said.

42

THE DAY 'MA' BARKER WAS SLAIN IN FLORIDA

OKLAWAHA—She was affectionately called "Ma," but my, my, what an unusual mother was Kate Barker! Born in the Ozarks, she was poor in her early years. So strong was her lust for money, furs and baubles, she turned to a life of crime and led her four young sons down the same path. The eldest, Herman, convinced her crime does pay, so she opened up in her own home a School of Crime for the younguns. When they were arrested for petty infractions, she upbraided them for getting caught. At one time, her alumni records showed Herman committing suicide rather than be arrested for murder; Arthur (Doc) was serving a life term for murder; Lloyd was in Leavenworth for 25 years for robbing the U.S. Mails, and Freddie was in Kansas State Pen for burglary and larceny.

"Ma" Barker acquired riches she wanted. In two kidnapings, her gang collected $300,000 in ransom. The FBI traced Ma and some of her gang to a lakeside retreat here on Lake Weir, in this beautiful, law-abiding community. The G-Men called for those inside the two-story frame cottage to surrender. A blaze of machine gun fire was the answer from the Barkers. Thus started a two-hour battle. The house was raked by bullets. Although it seemed like the whole gang was inside, only "Ma" and son Fred were doing all the shooting. They were found slain. This shootout took place Jan. 16, 1935.

The house still stands.

FLORIDA'S 'HOUSE OF SEVEN GABLES'

MAYO — "Half-way down a by-street of one of our New England towns, stands a rusty wooden house, with seven acutely-peaked gables, facing towards various points of the compass, and a huge, clustered chimney in the midst. . ."

Thus began Nathaniel Hawthorne's enduring self-labeled Romance, "The House of the Seven Gables," published in 1851.

Half way down a by-street in one of our North Florida towns, Mayo, to be exact, is a replica of the House of the Seven Gables and it was inspired by the famous story. This community is the county seat of Lafayette County, and is 28 miles east of Perry.

One block off U.S. Highway 27, at Clark and Bloxham Streets, sits the seven-gabled house. Local historians say it was erected around 1890.

The story goes that a Mayo resident named Jim Mitchell was fascinated by the description of the House of the Seven Gables in Hawthorne's romance and the idea grew in his mind that such a house would be ideal for his wife and brood. He went to a contractor named Mack Koon and closed a deal for the erection of this odd structure. It immediately became a "conversation piece" for the region in its early occupancy and has continued to be a "sight" for visitors to Mayo.

The building is in fairly good state of repair. The "gingerbread" along the eaves of the roof was hand-hewn.

44

SHE WROTE BOOKS IN SECLUSION OF QUAINT CROSS CREEK

CROSS CREEK—Folks over in Island Grove considered the people of Cross Creek just a little "biggety," according to the late Marjorie Kinnan Rawlings.

Island Grove sits astride U.S. 301 north of Ocala and sees much more of civilization than does this little fishing village four miles to the west. It is here that the charming novelist wrote many of her books, including the best seller "Cross Creek," which was her autobiography of life in backwoods Florida.

Author of three Book-of-the-Month selections ("South Moon Under," 1933; "The Yearling," 1939, and "Cross Creek," 1942), Mrs. Rawlings died December 14, 1953, at the age of 57. She won the Pulitzer Prize in 1939. She was married to Norton Baskin.

The author's 72-acre orange grove, which she operated, now belongs to the University of Florida Foundation, and is about the same as it was when she lived here.

Mrs. Rawlings' manuscripts and papers were left to the University's Library. At the University of Tampa in Tampa there is a "Marjorie Kinnan Rawlings Room" honoring the author. Rollins College awarded her an honorary doctorate in 1939 and Florida gave her a similar honor in 1941.

Despite being off the beaten path, Mrs. Rawlings' home attracts many tourists these days. Some peek to see if the noted outhouse which rated a whole chapter in "Cross Creek" still stands. No, it doesn't.

45

"DEM SPOOKS" PILOT CAR FOR YOU BACKING UPHILL

LAKE WALES— Throughout Florida, it's against the law to back a car more than 30 feet on a public street.

But in this lovely Polk County community the townspeople and officials encourage visiting motorists to back up on Fifth Avenue, as much as 75 to 100 feet. Other cars on the street "stack up" behind you and their occupants gleefully watch as your car goes backward up a steep hill—without your motor running.

If this sounds bewitching, it's because you're visiting Spook Hill. The way it works is this: Drive your car to the bottom of the hill, turn off your engine, release the brakes and clutch, and watch the Mystery of Spook Hill work for you. The car backs as much as 100 feet up the hill.

Your explanation of this phenomenon is as good as anyone's. The spiel which goes with this amusing experience is that an old Negro once parked his car at this spot so he could go fishing in nearby North Lake Wales. He looked back as he started for the lake and the smile froze on his face. His old jalopy was slowly moving back up the hill with the motor not running. "Dem Spooks!" cried the old man and fainted. This is how Spook Hill supposedly got its name.

And nearby Spook Hill School got its name from the hill!

'STEAMBOAT ARCHITECTURE' MARKS DeBARY MANSION

DeBARY—A poor Belgian immigrant who came to America in 1840 and became one of the country's wealthiest bon vivants left an attractive monument to his gay Florida days.

Baron Frederick DeBary struck it rich selling Mumm's Champagne and mineral waters. He was a charming fellow and made social friends of his big name customers. He entertained them in New York.

In his travels along the Eastern seaboard, Baron DeBary got captivated with pioneer Florida. He decided to develop a playground in the warm climate and selected a site on the north shore of the Lake Monroe section of the St. Johns River in Volusia County.

Besides building a mansion for entertaining friends, the Baron also fulfilled the desire of his sickly daughter Eugenie for a "pleasure palace." The adventurer considered this spot "the most desirable and beautiful location I have been able to find anywhere."

Completed in 1871, DeBary Hall rocked with merriment of gay parties for a long period. Presidents, princes and generals mingled with artists, actors and explorers at the estate. There were President U. S. Grant, General Robert E. Lee, President Grover Cleveland, Alexander Graham Bell, King Edward the VII when he was Prince of Wales, to name a few guests.

The Baron even operated two side wheeler steamboats to transport his visitors from Jacksonville to his plantation. The verandas circling the house gave it the look of "steamboat architecture."

DeBary died in 1898 at the age of 84. His mansion in 1959 became state headquarters for the Florida Federation of Art. It became a State Historic Memorial in 1967.

47

HOOVER DIKE PROTECTS 'BIG WATER' (LAKE OKEECHOBEE)

CLEWISTON—Okeechobee, as in Lake Okeechobee, is the colorfully descriptive name derived from two Indian words, meaning "big water."

The great body of water is a blessing to South Florida, but it also has been a curse. The lake went berserk twice in two years back in the 1920s when violent hurricanes roared into the Everglades section. National Geographic magazine described what happened to Lake Okeechobee after that mighty storm of 1928: "Fill a saucer with water, then sweep your hand through it and you will have some idea of the effect." The resulting flood killed between 1,500 and 2,500 persons. No accurate count was made, bodies were heaped in piles and buried.

Rushing here to the lake area was President Herbert Hoover, a shocked and saddened leader. According to an attractive marker on Hoover Dike here, the President "personally supported and was directly responsible for early Federal construction of Lake Okeechobee levees for the protection of life and property." Congress in 1960 designated the dike in commemoration of Hoover's "humanitarian efforts and interest in public safety, which permitted the safe development of the rich potential of this region."

Forty years in building, and costing more than $100 million, the 112 miles of 35-foot high Hoover Dike protect the people and the new land. The quaint local historian, Lawrence Will, reports: "The old-fashioned virtues of courage, fortitude and perseverence have transformed the former trap of death into a great agricultural empire, furnishing beef, vegetables and sugar for the nation's table."

FLORIDA BOASTS WORLD'S LARGEST CYPRESS TREE

LONGWOOD—It's ageless, it's enormous, it's interesting to study, it's distinctive among trees in that it was "dedicated" by the President of the United States of America!

Known as "The Senator" or "The Big Tree," this giant cypress stands straight and tall in a swamp between here and Sanford. It's been overlooking the landscape here since 1,000 or more years before the birth of Christ. The tree doesn't have a birth certificate, but it's estimated to be 3,500 years old.

Claiming to be the biggest cypress in the world, it also claims to be the largest tree in the Eastern United States. Let's measure it: "The Senator" now reaches 127 feet tall, but at one time it was 165 feet tall. A vicious Florida hurricane in 1926 clipped the top from the tree. In diameter, the Big Tree is 17 feet, and in circumference, 54 feet. It contains approximately 50,000 board feet, enough tough cypress wood to construct five small houses. It's so thick at the trunk it is wide enough for a roadway to be cut through.

This soft, tan colored tree got its name from Mose O. Overstreet, a state senator from 1920 to 1924, who donated land around the tree to Seminole County for a park. A few years later, in 1929, President Calvin Coolidge officially dedicated the site.

The Florida Forest Service reported recently that the Senator is recognized by the American Forestry Association as the largest living Pond Cypress and a champion on AFA's Social Register of Big Trees. In any event, The Senator has been a landmark around here since the Seminole first inhabited the area.

49

PERMANENT CHRISTMAS TREE
SYMBOL OF LOVE

CHRISTMAS—Santa Claus has a real helper in the lovely lady who attends to the chores of postmistress at this Florida village with the holiday name, located on State Road 50, 20 miles east of Orlando.

Mrs. Juanita Tucker not only sees that the floodtide of cards and packages that come to her post office each Christmas for postmarking are sent on their way promptly. But she also carries on a continuous promotion of the Christmas spirit in many ways.

She sparked a community drive to plant and decorate year round a colorful Christmas tree on the village green across from the famous little post office. It bears the inscription: "The permanent Christmas tree at Christmas, Fla., is the symbol of love and good will—the Christmas spirit every day of the year."

Mrs. Tucker wrote a little booklet called Christmas Every Day in which she describes the feeling in her community:

"At Christmas the nations of the earth meet in the spirit of love for God and man. The world is full of warm-hearted, kind people like those who visit Christmas. They come from all over the United States and many foreign countries. Every day it is Christmas for someone because of their love and thoughtfulness. Friend remembers friend... For a fleeting moment the spirit of Christmas is recaptured with all its elusive joy and expectancy; and the heart is warm and young again.

"This is Christmas, a simple little country village, typical of America."

Christmas, Fla., was the site for the first day of issue for the Christmas commemorative stamp in 1969.

50

HOW 'DUKE OF DUNNELLON' DISCOVERED PHOSPHATE

DUNNELLON—A small and quiet residential area is developing today along SR 40 near here where a hardy adventurer whose nickname was "The Duke of Dunnellon" discovered hard rock phosphate accidentally on May Day, 1889.

Albertus Vogt, engineer, U.S. Marshal, journalist, world traveler and adventurer, settled down here after his exciting experiences. He expected to grow oranges and enjoy hunting and fishing on the Withlacoochee River. But it happened that a remarkable incident changed the current of his life.

While sinking a well to supply water for his groves, Vogt discovered phosphate and the event began a new era in Central Florida. The "Dunnellon Formation" of hard rock phosphate extends as a narrow strip parallel with the Gulf coast from southern Suwannee and Columbia Counties to Hernando County. Vogt immediately took up options on all land in his district and afterward sold a half interest to John T. Dunn. Later Vogt sold his interest for $200,000. Dunnellon became a wild and lively "boom" town.

Florida's pebble phosphate industry, different from hard rock, had its start in 1884-85 when Capt. J. Francis Le Baron, an Army engineer, made the discovery in the bed of Peace River near Fort Meade.

(In photo, Dunnellon resident Billy Roland, descendant of a phosphate pioneer, studies historical marker designating the spot of Albertus Vogt's "lucky strike.")

51

PICTURESQUE HOMESTEAD REFLECTS PIONEER LIVING IN FLORIDA

STARKE—Less than a mile off busy U.S. 301 on the Brooker road is a pastoral scene that transforms the visitor to pioneer days of Florida.

This is the Mansell homestead featuring a rambling two-story structure which is the "old home place," built shortly after the Civil War. It's weather-beaten and in need of some attention, but is still liveable.

The interesting century-old home is owned by direct descendants of the pioneer Bradford County farmer who built it, Thomas Fletcher Mansell.

The frontiersman came here as a lad of 11 about 1856 from Pickens County, S. C. After the great conflict, he acquired the land from Hulda Prevatt, who had been widowed during the War.

Mansell built the home, at first just a one-story affair, but later a second story was added when the children came along. The kitchen and dining room, as was typical of the early days architecture, was separated from the living area by a crude "breezeway."

The hard-working pioneer planted an orange grove, some of the trees are still living despite the Big Freeze of the late 1880's. He also did general farming, raised cane, cotton, peanuts, sweet potatoes and other crops.

There are many relics of pioneer living on the place, including a king-sized well sweep and a cane-grinding apparatus that was operated with horse-power. Bradford County Telegraph Editor Gene Matthews has urged that the Mansell homestead be preserved for its historical value.

52

OCHOPEE, 'BIG FIELD,' HAS SMALLEST POST OFFICE

OCHOPEE—Isolated as she is, away down here on the Tamiami Trail, Ochopee nevertheless has a nationwide distinction. It has the littlest United States Post Office building.

Originally a tool shed, the structure measures seven foot, three inches by eight foot, four inches. It is so tiny that only one customer can squeeze in at a time, while Postmaster Sidney H. Brown efficiently serves his customers.

Presently the Post Office has 25 box holders, and a star route serving 40 residents operates from here. It rates as a third class post office.

Ochopee is just four miles south of the intersection of SR 29 and U.S. 41. The community bears an Indian name which has been interpreted to mean "Big Field," although Mr. Brown understands it means "Big Farm." Either monicker would have been appropriate back in the early 1930's when the town sprung up after the opening of Tamiami Trail in 1928 and huge tomato farms were planted here.

The town's founder was a Miami real estate developer, Capt. J. F. Jaudon, prime promoter of the Trail and who made the first survey of the road. He operated a sugar cane mill at Ochopee. And it was he, in 1932, who secured a Post Office for their own. Captain Jaudon served a year as Postmaster and then it was turned over to the good hands of Mr. Brown, under appointment from the new President, Franklin D. Roosevelt.

Postmaster Brown recalls that in 1932 Ochopee had more people than any other place in Collier County (Today Naples is county seat and its metropolitan area has about 17,000 inhabitants and is the fifth fastest growing city in Florida).

53

Florida West Coast

MECCA FOR MILLIONAIRES

TAMPA—Railroad magnate Henry B. Plant, builder of the elegant Tampa Bay Hotel, wired an invitation to rival railroad magnate Henry Flagler, who'd built plush hotels on the Florida East Coast.

"Where's the Tampa Bay?" coyly replied Flagler. "Follow the crowds," shot back Plant.

This was in 1891 and in the era following, the Tampa Bay became the mecca for presidents, cabinet members, legislators, European royalty, dozens of millionaires and many others from the international set.

The first housekeeper recalled in an interview years later:

"They came from all corners of the world in private cars and special trains to visit the Tampa Bay which was famed on two continents for its beauty, service and fine liquors . . . One large table in the dining room was reserved for 20 multi-millionaires . . . European royalty, including counts and countesses, often ate at one table . . ."

The Tampa Bay, now occupied by the University of Tampa, was Plant's hobby. He spent $3 million building it and nearly another million in furnishings. He sent Mrs. Plant to Europe with an unlimited drawing account to go on a shopping spree for furnishings.

The red brick structure, modeled after the Alhambra in Granada, Spain, is of Moorish architecture, two blocks long, four stories high, 500 rooms, and spread over an area of six acres.

(In 1963, Holiday magazine called it an "eyesore;" a short time later, State Rep. Robert Mann, of Tampa, complained about it being "an ugly view.")

Plant died in 1899. The hotel was sold to the city of Tampa in 1905 and was operated until 1929. It became the university in 1933. The building was U.S. Army headquarters during the Spanish-American War. Teddy Roosevelt camped nearby.

EDISON LAUNCHED FORT MYERS' 'AVENUE OF PALMS'

FORT MYERS—This tropical paradise in South Florida lives up to its name, "The City of Palms."

It was the inventive genius, Thomas A. Edison, who settled here in the town's pioneer days of 1885, and launched the project that began a citywide palm planting.

McGregor Boulevard, which bisects his Winter home estate here, is famous as one of the most beautiful avenues of palms in the world. The inventor brought these original palms in from the island of Cuba in 1900 and planted two miles of them on this avenue. There was a plentiful supply of the Royal Palms growing wild about 60 miles south of Fort Myers at the edge of the Everglades. But when Edison started his beautification program it was easier to bring the trees by sailboat from Cuba than by ox teams through the dense Florida swamps. McGregor Boulevard now has over 15 miles of palms.

More than 70 different varieties of tropical palms grow here. The official palm count is 10,752—on city land and right of way.

Edison was a booster of his adopted city and prophesied, "There's only one Fort Myers—and 90 million people are going to find it out."

After Edison built an electric light plant on his grounds, he reportedly offered to install free lights in the town, provided the community would furnish the poles. The town council turned down the offer, because the lights might keep the cattle awake. But while he was in his residence, Edison brilliantly illuminated his grounds with the new incandescent electric light.

EDISON FLORIDA HOME FIRST PRE-FAB HOUSE

FORT MYERS—Thomas A. Edison discovered Fort Myers while searching for a filament for the incandescent lamp which he perfected later. He also found a spot to spend his Winters—and to regain his health.

In March, 1885, the great inventor and a friend came upriver from Punta Rassa to see the tropical bamboo which thrived here. Within 24 hours, the "Yankee visitor" was a property owner here and for nearly 50 years, until his death in 1931, he spent his winters in a lovely home. Incidentally, he didn't use bamboo filament in the lamp.

Edison went back north and drew plans for his dream home down in Florida. He had the home and breezeway-connected guest house built in sections in Fairfield, Maine. The next year he shipped them to Fort Myers via four schooners. They actually were among the first pre-fabricated houses in history!

The inventor's widow deeded the house, gardens and laboratories to the City of Fort Myers in 1947 to be maintained as a monument in his honor. They're open to the public.

A wide veranda goes around the main part of the houses to keep out rain. No windows but only doors are in the lower part of the houses. The home is divided into two houses because Edison did not like the smell of food or the heat of cooking and the kitchen and dining area were made separate.

On the fabulous estate, Edison constructed the first swimming pool built in Florida, reinforcing it with bamboo instead of steel. It has never had a crack or a leak. A rare botanical garden with more than 300 species of shrubs and trees, imported from all over the world, greet visitors. Edison's next door neighbor was Henry Ford.

57

PENSACOLA BOASTS OLDEST CHURCH BUILDING IN STATE

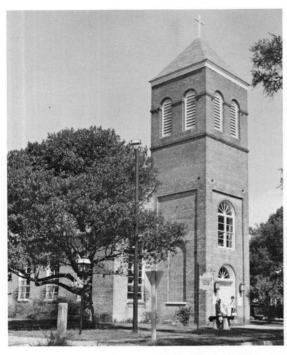

PENSACOLA — Historic Old Christ Church is one of the oldest church buildings still standing on its original site in Florida. The handsome Episcopal structure was completed in 1832.

The church, now used as a historical museum, was modeled after Christopher Wren's Old North Church of Boston, where lanterns flashed to warn "The British are coming." It is said that the Pensacola church was built from plans supplied by Sir Christopher Wren.

First rector was the son of the Senior Warden of Christ Church, Philadelphia. The first child christened in the church was Lucy Barklay who later became the organist and choir directress of the church.

The attractive brick used in erecting the structure was kilned locally at Bright Brick Plant. Visitors quickly notice the giant hand-hewn heart pine beams of the ceiling, which are in the form of an inverted ship's hull, the simplest and safest roof structure at the time.

The Union forces took over the church during the Civil War and reportedly used it for a hospital, barracks and stable. Three Episcopal ministers are buried beneath the floor.

When the parish moved to new quarters in 1903, the building was then used by the Negro Episcopal congregation for several years. In 1936 the church became the City Library and then in 1960 the museum.

The church is beautifully lit at night and is a striking picture overlooking Seville Square where Creek Indians paraded American scalps after the Fort Mims massacre in Alabama in 1814.

58

FORT SAN CARLOS' YO-YO OWNERSHIP

PENSACOLA—On the reservation of the U.S. Naval Air Station here stands the sturdy Fort San Carlos, whose colorful history dates back to the earliest development of Florida, and has had many "owners."

As the Spanish sought to strengthen their position in the new world, a colonial expedition led by Adm. Don Andres de Arriola landed in the mid-1690's. The body of 300 soldiers immediately built Fort San Carlos, naming it in honor of Spain's King Charles II.

The French, keen rivals of the Spanish, touched down at Pensacola about this time but moved along to settle in Mississippi and New Orleans. This co-existence didn't last long. In 1719, as war raged in Europe, the French surprised the Spaniards in Pensacola, who capitulated. But the Spanish got reinforcements from Havana and Fort San Carlos was recaptured. Subsequently, however, the French regained Pensacola in a bloody battle. The fort was burned in the process. Finally, the city was restored to Spanish control in 1723.

England erected a fort on the site in 1771, but it was destroyed by the Spanish when they regained West Florida in 1783. A new San Carlos was built, a massive 100 x 100 foot semi-circular fort built of handmade bricks with a dry moat, and finished in 1790. In 1814 it was lost to the English and then to the United States, who returned it to Spain after the War of 1812.

The historic fort was again taken for the U.S. in 1818, after an Indian uprising, by doughty Gen. Andrew Jackson.

59

'CRADLE TO GRAVE' MILITIA
GALLANTLY DEFENDED MARIANNA

MARIANNA — One of the memorable raids of the Civil War was made on this historic community.

In a way, it was ironic that the Federals would make it so hot for Marianna. One historian said: "The quiet little town, undeserving of such a visitation by Federal troops, for it had been noted before secession as a center of Unionist sentiment, was the scene of a fierce hand-to-hand fight."

It was on Sept. 27, 1864, that a band of U.S. raiders led by Gen. Asboth, approached this Jackson County capital. Colonel Montgomery had headquarters for Confederate units posted at neighboring points.

Quickly, the alarm spread and small boys from the town and nearby plantations went into action, along with old men and disabled soldiers who were convalescing here. They were armed with shotguns and rifles, and barricaded the street.

General Asboth arrived, attacking from front and rear, and he set fire to the buildings upon which the Home Guard depended largely for protection.

One account of the day's events said: "When the musketry was still and the flames had died down, a ghastly spectacle was presented. The charred remains of some of the boys who had fought at the barricade were found among the ruins. About 60 soldiers and citizens were casualties. Many of the victims were buried in the cemetery of the St. Luke's Episcopal Church around which the battle raged."

Today, a striking monument stands proudly in the center of Marianna on U.S. 90 to mark the Battle of Marianna.

60

STATE PARK NOW SITE FOR RESTORED MANSION

TORREYA STATE PARK—A fine example of ante-bellum architecture is the beautifully restored Gregory House, now a feature of Torreya State Park off Florida 12 between Bristol and Chattahoochee.

The attractive mansion sits majestically atop Neal's Bluff facing the Apalachicola River. But it hasn't always been here.

Once upon a time there was a county known as Fayette, named in honor of the Marquis de Lafayette. It was created in 1832 by the Territorial Legislature and was abolished just two years later. The capital of Fayette was the town of Ocheesee.

An affluent settler here was Jason Gregory, who acquired much acreage and engaged in cotton farming, which was shipped down the river. He built this aristocratic two-story house in 1834.

The Gregory House figured in events of the Civil War. There was a river gun-boat, the Chattahoochee, that patrolled the river and the crews often were guests at the luxurious home. The boat sank at Blountstown in 1863 and the wounded were evacuated to the Gregory House until they could be transferred. One victim in the explosion was the son of the Confederate Secretary of Navy Stephen R. Mallory.

The last big social event in this mansion was the marriage of Ida Gregory, the oldest daughter, to William Falke during Christmas, 1865. The Gregory family fled the area in 1873 to escape yellow fever. They moved to Gainesville, and even so, all the family save daughter Chaffa died in the epidemic. She returned to the old home and lived there until her death. It was sold, finally donated to the State and moved.

61

INDIANS FROLICKED
AT FLORIDA PLAYGROUND

FORT WALTON BEACH—This delightful section of Florida is heralded as the "Playground Area" and it is just that for numerous tourists who enjoy the beaches and other recreational facilities.

But, going back hundreds of years, there is evidence the Indians fell in love with the Gulf Coast to relax and play. And right here on main street in the heart of town today stands the most accessible large Indian Temple Mound on the coast of North America. It covers more than an acre of ground and it took more than 500,000 basket loads of earth to build. The primitive red men constructed it by manual labor over a long period of years.

During the so-called Fort Walton Culture (1300 A.D. to 1700 A.D.) the Temple Mound was the swinging civic, social and religious center of the Indian tribes, which came from all over northwest Florida and Southern Alabama.

The Indians of that culture buried their dead in cemeteries, but some burials have been discovered in the Mound, probably of Indians in later periods. There was an excavation in 1861 and at a depth of 18 inches there were found, "Great skeletons of men in perfect state of preservation . . . They crossed each other and were filled with a four-inch layer of preserving matter, a mixture of lime and some other mineral substance." Confederate soldiers removed the skeletons, displayed them at their fort which was burned later.

The Temple Mound property was acquired by the City of Fort Walton Beach in 1959. It is a national landmark designated by the U.S. Secretary of the Interior. An interesting museum also is operated here.

REAL ROYALTY ONCE GRACED FLORIDA'S CAPITAL

TALLAHASSEE—He was a nephew of Napoleon Bonaparte and she was a grandniece of George Washington. They were married by a Justice of Peace in Tallahassee on July 12, 1824, and lived happily the rest of their lives. Today, the bodies of the royal pair rest in old St. Johns Episcopal cemetery.

Charles Louis Napoleon Achille Murat, the prince, was son of Napoleon's sister and her husband who was King of Naples. Exiled by both France and Italy, the glamorous prince wound up in Florida at the behest of Lafayette.

The prince—who resembled his handsome, famous uncle—fell in love with a young widow, Catherine Willis Gray, who lived in Pensacola. Her father was a close friend of Andrew Jackson.

The royal couple built a country home, "Lipona," in Jefferson County which became the social center of the area. The prince was a learned man and traveled much. At one time after their marriage he was commander of Belgium King Leopold's "Foreign Legion." When he bade his troops goodbye, he addressed them in seven different languages. He also was active in the Seminole War in Florida and was a friend of many Indian chiefs. Prince Murat served as mayor and postmaster of Tallahassee and as county judge of Jefferson County.

But one historian recorded that it was Murat's fate to be remembered in Florida for his omniverous appetite. The story goes that the only exception he made among all available creatures that crawled, swam or flew, was "ze turkey boozard." He died in 1847 at the age of 47. The princess moved into another home, Belle vue, which still stands, now displayed at the Junior Museum. She died in 1867.

63

POLITICAL GIANTS DREW
FIRST CONSTITUTION

PORT ST. JOE—There have been few bodies of men chosen in America more competent than the 56 delegates who framed Florida's first Constitution.

So wrote historian W. T. Cash in describing the architects of the Constitution of 1838. For 34 working days—including Christmas and New Year's Day—they debated as they hammered out the basic law in the period between December 3, 1838, and January 11, 1839.

The pioneers were getting Florida in shape to be admitted to the Union, an act which did not happen until 1845 due to the national squabble over slave and free states' admissions.

The booming frontier town of St. Joseph next door to present day Port St. Joe (on scenic U.S. 98) was the site of this historic drafting session. Today an impressive Museum at the State Constitution Memorial at Port St. Joe contains interpretive exhibits of the event and contemporary history.

Scraps between East Florida and West Florida and between the Whigs and the Democrats featured such greats as William P. Duval, David Levy Yulee, Robert Raymond Reid and many others. The final vote was 55 to 1. A referendum was held and the result was so tight the returns were not made public for nearly two years. A majority of 119 favored the Constitution.

St. Joseph faded into obscurity shortly after its moment in history, unable to survive a deadly yellow fever epidemic and destructive hurricanes in 1841 and 1844.

YOU 'WALLOW IN HISTORY' AT ST. MARKS!

ST. MARKS—A woman writer from the North visited ancient San Marcos de Apalache here a few years ago and exclaimed: "you simply wallow in history when you go to St. Marks!"

Indeed, you do. The history of this coastal defense town goes back long before the arrival of white man in the Western Hemisphere. The first visitor from Europe was that daring Spanish explorer, Panfilo de Narvaez, who fought Indians through Florida swamps all the way from Tampa Bay up to this port in the Panhandle. He scrapped them here, too, in 1527, to the exasperation point and he was anxious to get moving. He beat his swords into tools and his company of 300 followers constructed five small ships, thus starting the first ship-building industry in Florida. They shipped out, disappearing in the Gulf of Mexico never to be seen again.

Hernando de Soto followed in de Narvaez' footsteps. Other Spaniard explorers, soldiers and missionaries came later, all harrassed by the pirates and the Indians and later the British. Wooden forts were first built but in 1739 a limestone fort was erected and remnants of it still exist at what is now a State Park here.

In the year 1800, a British deserter, William Augustus Bowles, who had married an Indian squaw, took the fort and set himself up as "King of Florida." His reign was short-lived as the fort was recaptured shortly by the Spanish. In 1818, Andrew Jackson captured the place as an aftermath of the War of 1812 stirring an international incident which nearly provoked war.

65

FLORIDA'S OLDEST INHABITED COMMUNITY

CRYSTAL RIVER—The archaelogists just love Crystal River! So do fishermen, hunters, tourists and others. The area is attractive today, just as it was—now hear this—10,000 to 13,000 years ago!

The digging fraternity started in 1902 trying to dig up the ancient history obviously planted here for centuries. They have come up with enough now for the State of Florida to erect a beautiful museum and to develop a State Park on land furnished by George Dyer, who besides being a lawyer and real estate man is some sort of a history bug.

The evidence is in that ancient Indian tribes romped on the shores of Crystal River as far back as 11,000 B.C., that's right, Before Christ. They've found arrow-heads here of the Suwannee variety used by the Paleo Indians around 10,000 B.C. The Crystal River site, as it is properly identified, is regarded as the second most important archaelogical site in the whole of North and South America, the first most important being located in Peru.

The museum is located just off U.S. 19-98 immediately north of the town of Crystal River near the Gulf of Mexico. There are interesting burial mounds on the site, and the middens where the Indians buried their refuse, and, of course, there are temple mounds.

Among the highly unusual mementoes of the past here are two stelae—stone slabs used for commemorative purposes. These are the only known stone stelae in the U.S., and ties us back in history to Mexico.

OLD HOTEL TYPIFIES SLEEPY FISHING VILLAGE

CEDAR KEY—One of Florida's most picturesque communities is this fishing village 22 miles off U.S. 19 midway between Tampa and Tallahassee. Easy does it is the way of life here.

Headquarters for peace-seekers and lazy vacationers is the old Island Hotel in the heart of "downtown." It's not known just how old the weather-beaten structure is, but it's over 125 years old. Now operated by Mrs. Bessie Gibbs, who also has been the town's mayor, it is known far and wide for its outstanding food, featuring native dishes such as swamp cabbage salad, and turtle steaks.

For years Cedar Key was under the "curse" slapped on her by the railroad magnate, Henry B. Plant. Back in the 1880s, when Cedar Key was a swingin' place, had a population of 5000 and the second largest port in Florida, Plant wanted to build a railroad here. He was stopped cold by Florida's first U.S. Senator, David Levy Yulee, who already had a railroad operating here and controlled much of the land. Plant fumed: "I'll wipe Cedar Key off the map! Owls will hoot in your attics and hogs will wallow in your deserted streets!" He came to Tampa, instead, and triggered development there.

Cedar Key once was the home of pencil factories of Eberhard Faber, but the cedar supply ran out due to exploitation of timber resources. Indians and pirates once lived in this and the other 99 keys in the group.

FIRST U.S. SENATOR LOST SUGAR MILL IN CIVIL WAR

HOMOSASSA—There is much to see in the ruins of a large sugar mill that was constructed here in 1851 by one of Florida's first U.S. Senators, David Levy Yulee.

Persons turning off U.S. 19-98 at Homosassa Springs see at this historic site the large limestone chimney, the old boiler set, the crushing machinery, the large cogwheel and portions of the engines. The mill was destroyed during the Civil War. At one time the plantation covered 100 acres. The property, now owned by the State, at one time was owned by the Citrus County Federation of Women's Clubs.

David Levy was a native of the British West Indies. His grandfather had been a Grand Vizier to the Sultan in the Moroccan Court; his grandmother was an English Jewess. Yulee was the Moorish name used by Levy's grandfather. Levy County, next door to Citrus, is named in his honor.

Young Levy came to Florida with his family while the state was under the Spanish rule. He participated in the first Constitutional Convention and was a Territorial Delegate to Congress. He was our first U.S. Senator. He had his name changed to Yulee by an act of the Legislature after his Senatorial election.

The Senator was an ardent secessionist and left the Senate on Jan. 21, 1861. At various times he lived in Florida at St. Augustine, Fernandina, Homosassa and Archer. After the war, he was imprisoned in Ft. Pulaski for aiding in the escape of Jefferson Davis.

In 1880 the erstwhile Senator moved to Washington. He died in New York City on Oct. 10, 1886, at the age of 76.

JOSE MARTI, CUBA'S 'GEORGE WASHINGTON,' SLEPT HERE

TAMPA—Ybor City, Tampa's colorful Latin quarter, was a place of intrigue during the buildup to and during the Spanish-American War. An exciting rendezvous for the revolutionaries was the Cherokee Club, an attractive red brick building at the northwest corner of 9th Ave. and 14th St. where it still stands.

This was the second brick building in Ybor City and was erected in 1888. It soon became the meeting place for the elite, and later became known as El Pasaje Restaurant.

Jose Marti, the leader of the Cuban insurrection in 1895, slept at this hotel on his first trip to Tampa, Nov. 25, 1891. Before retiring he said, "I feel happy amongst warriors."

During the Spanish American War other big names often were seen at the El Pasaje. There were Col. "Teddy" Roosevelt, Sir Winston Churchill, President Grover Cleveland, Gen. Leonard Wood and others. From 1890 to 1935 all Governors of Florida were feted here.

There are other memorable spots in Ybor City marking Marti's stay. Across the street from the El Pasaje is still standing the pioneer cigar factory on the front steps of which Marti made a speech of liberation in 1893. Next door to the old restaurant is the Cuban club and a bust of Marti is erected on the corner. A Jose Marti Park is at 8th Ave. and 13th St., at the spot where Marti stayed at La Casa de Pedroso, the house of Paulina Pedroso, great woman patriot of Cuba. The official newspaper of the Cuban revolutionary party was published nearby.

69

SITE OF BLOODY DADE MASSACRE NOW A PARK

BUSHNELL—A block or so off busy U.S. 301 in Bushnell is a quiet and peaceful State Park, designated Dade Battlefield Historic Memorial.

It was under the shady oaks which today provide an umbrella for picnickers that one of the bloodiest battles ever fought in Florida took place a couple days after Christmas in 1836.

This is where a detachment of U.S. soldiers, being transferred from Fort Brooke (Tampa) to Fort King (Ocala) was slaughtered by furious Seminole Indians on rampage, in a surprise attack. The massacre of gallant Maj. Francis L. Dade and his command triggered the Second Seminole War, or Florida War as it is sometimes called.

The white men were first assaulted at 8 A.M.; half of the command fell dead or wounded at the first fire. The Indians were frightened away by fire from a cannon. Then a lull ensued.

During this quiet, some of the soldiers felled pine trees with which they constructed a triangular breastwork. Their crude fortification was only knee-high (see replica in photo) when the Indians attacked again and finished wiping out all but two of the group of 100.

Major Dade's memory was honored by the naming of newly-created Dade County a few weeks later, and again with the naming of the town of Dade City, a few miles south of the park on U.S. 301.

70

HOME TOWN HONORS DR. JOHN GORRIE

APALACHICOLA—One of the two Floridians occupying niches in the Nation's Capitol building in Washington is Dr. John Gorrie, whose statue is in Statuary Hall.

But the famed doctor is not without honor in his home town here. There's an important museum which recognizes Dr. Gorrie and his contribution to mankind—the invention of the first ice making machine.

As a young physician, Dr. Gorrie settled here in 1833 at a time when Apalachicola thrived as a cotton-shipping port. His biggest challenge was caring for patients suffering from malaria. While searching for ways to bring down the fever of his patients, he devised a primitive system of air-conditioning, making use of natural ice shipped in from the Great Lakes. Then he started working on machines to make ice. He patented his invention in 1851.

Of course, such a far-fetched idea as this brought ridicule from many quarters, including the northern press which charged, "There's a crank down in Apalachicola, Florida, who claims that he can make ice as good as God Almighty!"

Dr. Gorrie spent his own fortune on the invention, and died in 1855, at the age of 52, a disillusioned and humiliated man. He was a beloved and popular citizen of Apalachicola, serving the community in many ways other than professionally. He was elected Intendant (Mayor) in 1837 and directed a progressive administration. He was a leading member of old Trinity Episcopal Church, most active in the Masonic Lodge and other activities.

THE OLD INDIAN TRADING POST ON STILTS

CHOKOLOSKEE—A modern causeway built in 1956 brought this picturesque tropical isle within reach of the motoring public. One of the tiniest of the Ten Thousand Islands, its mounds prove it was occupied by Indians in the ancient days. Civilization has come to "Chuckaluskee"—as the natives pronounce it—even the water bus to carry youngsters to school has been discontinued.

One of the landmarks that has been here for years remains the same today as it did back before the turn of the century. It is Smallwood's Store, an old Indian trading post, which for decades provided local residents and the nearby Seminoles with necessities of life and offered post office service to this isolated village six miles south of Everglades (which itself is four miles west of U.S. 41).

The store was opened by C. S. "Ted" Smallwood in 1906. Its main customers were the Indians who traded their alligator hides, game and berries from the Everglades, for calico and sugar. The pioneer, a native of Columbia County in North Florida, also took over the duties of postmaster from another hardly islander, C. G. McKinney. The post office dates back to 1891 when the water-locked community was known as "Comfort." A severe storm in 1924 alerted Smallwood to the dangers of water to his property and he raised the building on stilts as it now stands. Thus it escaped the disastrous 1926 hurricane.

Smallwood's daughter, Miss Thelma Smallwood, is operator of the interesting general store today. It is crammed to the rafters with basic supplies, including tin pails, wooden buckets, kerosene lamps, candies in glass display jars, all of which gives the rustic enterprise that "old fashioned look."

WALKING DREDGE HAD ROLE IN BUILDING TAMIAMI TRAIL

COLLIER SEMINOLE STATE PARK—Probably no rougher terrain ever challenged man's engineering ingenuity in roadbuilding more than did the swampy Florida Everglades in the construction of the Tamiami Trail.

Overcoming obstacle after obstacle, disappointment after disappointment, discouragement after discouragement, the hardy and heroic pioneers conquered swamplands and rugged rock deposits and laid down a ribbon of asphalt to link Miami with the Florida West Coast. Gov. John W. Martin, a road-building governor, dedicated the Trail on April 28, 1928, 13 years after the idea was first seriously considered· Its cost has been variously reported from seven million to 13 million dollars.

One of the persevering contractors on the job explained it took three "m's" to build the road—"men, money and machinery." And another observer facetiously paraphrased the three m's to mean "muck, misery and moccasins." A writer cited the Trail project as a classic example of "hell and highwater."

A sentimental memento of the tools used to build the Trail is preserved in a prominent spot at the entrance to Collier Seminole State Park, which is about 20 miles south of Naples on the Trail (U.S. 41). It is called a "walking dredge" which crawled its way through the Everglades and contributed so much toward the construction of the project.

The plaque on the primitive 20-ton monster explains its role: "THIS BAY CITY WALKING DREDGE IN CHARGE OF EARL W. IVEY AND MEECE ELLIS WORKING 18 HOURS DAILY, CONSTRUCTED THAT PORTION OF THE TAMIAMI TRAIL BEGINNING AT BLACK WATER RIVER AND EXTENDING NORTHWESTERLY 10 MILES TO BELLE MEADE CROSSING, AND ADJOINING THIS PARK IN 1927-28."

73

SANIBEL LIGHT GUARDS
ISLAND PARADISE

SANIBEL ISLAND—Frederic Babcock, a former travel writer for the Chicago Tribune, who roamed some 50 countries over five continents in his journalistic journeys, discovered what old timers on this Gulf Coast isle knew all along:

"If there is a perfect climate or a perfect place to live, I failed to find it. But Sanibel is as near to that ideal as I ever encountered."

The "privacy" of the natives was invaded somewhat in 1963 when a four million dollar bridge and causeway opened up this idyllic spot to more folk. It's still a quiet retreat stretching 20 miles along with its sister island, Captiva, and about two miles wide. It is rated as one of the world's topmost shelling areas, and lies 18 miles west of Ft. Myers on the Gulf of Mexico.

Once the playground and hideout of such pirates as Jose Gaspar and Black Caesar and Calico Jack, Sanibel was taken over by the U.S. government in 1821 and the cutthroats were chased away. The interesting lighthouse, with its brown square pyramidal skeleton tower, enclosing stair cylinder, was erected in 1884. Its bright light sweeps out 16 miles to sea. One of the early keepers was Henry Shanahan and his son Gene, who tended the kerosene light in the old days for 26 years.

After the pirates were shaken, first settlers came in 1830 and in 1833, Florida real estate promoters started their first "subdivision" on the island, putting up a few houses and paved streets. They incorporated the communities of Murray and Senybal, but the towns were shortlived. They were destroyed during the Indian Wars.

SUNSHINE AND BENCHES

ST. PETERSBURG—St. Petersburg's sunshine and green benches combine to create the illusion that life gets off to a good start at 75, not 40. So says an account of this city's trademarks.

The green benches, which have provided curbside perches for winter visitors for more than 60 years, are on the way out under orders of the City Council. But the city fathers decreed new resting places must be made of aluminum tubing and natural finish wooden slats of either Douglas fir or clear heart redwood "dressed, free of knots and splinters."

Father of the famous benches was Noel Mitchell, who came here from Rhode Island and went into the real estate business (doesn't everyone?). He purchased the two-story wooden Durant Building at Fourth and Central, site of the Rutland Building today. His ground floor offices became the hangout for idle tourists who appreciated his comfortable chairs. But the office became too crowded to work in.

Mitchell came up with the idea of constructing comfortable benches on the sidewalks. Other merchants followed suit. Everybody was happy. In 1914, Mayor Al Lang proclaimed the benches to be painted green.

One writer described them, thusly: "These slatted divans serve as mediums of introduction, with the weather the opening and principal topic. Operations, symptons, and remedies run a close second. The benches are the open-air offices of the promoter, the hunting grounds of the real estate 'bird dog,' a haven for the lonely, and a matrimonial bureau for many. They have figured in fiction, swindles, and divorce courts."

ARTISTIC RINGLING HOME, NOW NEW COLLEGE

SARASOTA—Charles Ringling was one of a more conservative temperament than others among the seven famous Ringling Brothers. He devoted his energy to the business and artistic elements of the Circus, carrying on the advertising and helping create music for the show.

When his brother John settled here, Charles acquired property to the north of John's estate and built for his wife, Edith, a marble palace. Charles lived in it only a year before his death in 1926. The widow raised their two children and the family enjoyed the spacious home through the years until her death in 1953.

Today, this handsome building partly houses New College, an unique approach to higher education, which moved in 1962. The house is now converted so that it serves as the library.

The Music Room is equipped with a pipe organ and piano which were used in the Ringling days by this musically talented family. The piano, it is said, was flown down to Sarasota by Ford tri-motored plane for a house concert at which Mme. Schumann Heink appeared. The music stand was used by Fritz Kreisler.

Throughout the building are magnificent pieces of furniture. In the Reception Hall is Mrs. Ringling's Church Pew, a 15th Century piece; there's also a Renaissance Cabinet in the hall. The house was designed by Clas, Shepard and Clas of Milwaukee.

ALL LAND SURVEYS IN FLORIDA BEGIN AT THIS POINT

TALLAHASSEE—At an obscure spot near the city jail here is a concrete monument that marks the beginning of all land surveys in Florida. It is the intersection of the guide meridian and the base parallel for the state.

The site dates back to the territorial days of Florida when Tallahassee was first selected as the capital city. It was while William P. Duval was Territorial Governor that he received a notice from the Government Land Office in Washington announcing the appointment of Col. Robert A. Butler of Tennessee to be surveyor general of Florida. The communication was dated July 10, 1824.

Colonel Butler was directed to select a point of beginning for all surveys, and from this the townships and ranges were to be numbered. Selection of the survey point really revolved around the location of the Capitol building since it was desired to locate the seat of government in the center of the quarter section. The monument, hence, is situated in a low, wet area about 1,500 feet south and east of the Capitol.

The Colonel drove down a lightwood post to mark the key spot. Many years passed and in 1853, the State Legislature voted to require the Governor to place a stone with a suitable inscription at the spot. Governor Broome ignored the legislative order and it was not until 1892 that a permanent type marker was placed. The present stone monument was authorized by the 1925 Legislature.

A capital observer, Angus Laird, has reported there is some dispute whether the stone marker is at the exact spot where the original lightwood post was sunk, but no legal significance is attached to the discrepancy if indeed there is a difference.

DR. BRADEN BUILT A CASTLE

BRADENTON—Dr. Joseph Addison Braden was a pioneer settler in this area. A native of Virginia, he came from Tallahassee to Manatee River in 1843 and acquired a 1100-acre sugar plantation.

He built a sugar mill, but his masterpiece edifice was his "castle" near the confluence of the Manatee and Braden rivers in East Bradenton. Using slave labor and materials at hand, Dr. Braden erected a 2½ story building with eight large rooms, spacious halls, four large chimneys and eight fireplaces. The walls were made of an odd material: "Tabby," composed of lime, sand, crused oyster and clam shells and water, molded into large bricks. The roofless remains of the castle make an interesting study today. The wood used was obtained from the property, oak, hickory and pine. The windows and doors came from Mobile. Begun in 1845, it was completed in 1851.

Pioneer citizens of the region often sought refuge from the Indians in this sturdy castle. In 1856, a party of seven Indians attacked the castle, but Dr. Braden returned the fire with Major Gamble's new repeating rifle, wounding one Indian.

When Union soldiers destroyed Dr. Braden's sugar mill and freed his slaves, he abandoned the property, in 1864. Two years later Gen. James G. Cooper obtained the Braden property and lived in the castle until his death. He added a cupola from which an excellent view of the section was obtained. A woods fire in 1903 destroyed the building, except for the walls. The castle was sold to the Camping Tourists of America in 1924, by Cooper's grandson, J. J. Pelot. Braden Castle Camp today is a trailer park.

When the post office was established in 1878, a spelling error made it "Braidentown." In 1924, the "i" and the "w" were dropped.

78

SITE OF KORESHAN CULT NOW STATE PARK

ESTERO—Cyrus Reed Teed dreamed big. He envisioned that one day Estero would be larger than Chicago or New York, that it would have a population of eight to ten million. Its streets would be 400 feet wide.

For this was the "New Jerusalem" for his cult, known as the Koreshan Unity. Fantastic as were some of its beliefs, Dr. Teed had a following, though much smaller in number than he had expected would flock to him.

The vision of himself as a new messiah came one night in 1869, back in Utica, N.Y. This was the seed for a new religion. He decided that while the world is round, as Columbus discovered, the fact is we live **inside** of the earth. People are like seeds in a grapefruit. Teed operated a non-atheistic communistic community, his followers signing over all their worldly good to him. He also required celibacy and separated the sexes.

After operating from Chicago for a while, he came to this lower Gulf coast community in 1894 and eventually acquired several hundred acres of property for his cult.

Teed died on Dec. 22, 1908. His followers refused to bury him because he had preached he would rise again. A day or so after Christmas local health authorities ordered the messiah interred anyway. His followers buried him under a concrete slab at the end of Fort Myers Beach. In 1921 a hurricane swept away his remains. Today the art center is one building left and the property has become a State Park.

JUST A LITTLE BIT OF A PLACE

SARASOTA—There's a huge life-size painting of John Ringling in the entrance way of his fabulous Ca'D'Zan. It's a good likeness of the circus king, but his pal Will Rogers wasn't convinced when he visited the Sarasota palace.

"That's a mighty fine painting, Mr. Ringling, but it's not a bit like you; it's not characteristic," drawled the comedian.

Pressed to explain, Will quipped, "Because you've got your hand in your own pocket!"

Everything else about the House of John is characteristic: It depicts wealth, good taste, imagination, color and a bit of showmanship. Really, Ringling himself hadn't cared for a mansion. Said he: "I would be satisfied with just a little bit of a place."

But his beautiful wife Mable wanted an outstanding structure, one that would remind her of Venice she adored so much. Guess who won? It cost more than $1,500,000 to build and furnish. The Ringlings moved into their home which dominate a 36-acre estate on Christmas Day, 1926. But their happiness was short-lived. Mrs. Ringling died three years later of Addison's disease.

John Ringling remarried and later divorced. He died in 1936. His estate was willed to the State of Florida. The second Mrs. Ringling contested. She got $1, the State got the valuable properties.

NAPOLEON'S AIDE SETTLED, 'GOD'S OWN RESTING PLACE'

SAFETY HARBOR—Dr. Odet Phillipi was the first white settler and grandfather of the first white child born in this region. His grave site overlooks Tampa Bay, which was known as Espiritu Santo Bay in 1823.

Dr. Phillipi was directed here by a pirate he had befriended and who said of Tampa Bay: "If there is a God, surely this is His resting place. There is but one bay to compare with it, Naples . . ."

Count Phillipi was a great nephew of Louis XVII and friend of Napoleon Bonaparte, who appointed him chief surgeon of the French armed forces. The British captured and imprisoned him and then later freed him after his heroic action in a yellow fever epidemic. He made his way to South Carolina and joined the French Huguenots.

He pulled stakes there in 1819, wound up in the Indian River region of Florida and was credited with originating the now famous Indian River citrus. Fearing an Indian uprising, he fled four years later. On the voyage his ship was intercepted by the pirates, who gave him the "Chamber of Commerce pitch" on Tampa Bay.

Dr. Phillipi cultivated a 100-acre grove, which was destroyed in 1848 by a hurricane and tidal wave. During the Civil War, he and his family moved to Hernando County. After the war he returned to his old hammock and plantation called St. Helena.

In his sunset years he sat by the waters he loved and reflected on the past and Napoleon. He would say: "This is God's own country, and this water His medicine, stirred by His hand, and deposited on this shore to heal man's suffering." He died in 1869.

'THE CHAUTAUQUA THAT BEGAN UNDER A TREE'

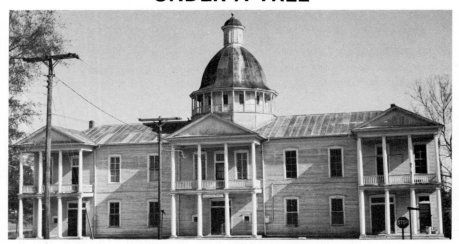

DeFUNIAK SPRINGS—The stately building with the "town hall look" that graces the shore of the beautiful lake here once housed the second oldest Chautauqua in the United States. Credited with being a founder of the unit here is Bishop John H. Vincent himself, the man who started the religious and educational movement at Chautauqua, N. Y.

The local institution was referred to as the "Chautauqua that began under a tree" because the organizers met under a large oak to discuss plans for the building. It was incorporated in 1885. Col. William D. Chipley, the big railroad man, for whom the town of Chipley in Washington County is named, interested railroad and steamship lines in the project and brought excursion groups here.

The first State Teachers Association and County Superintendents convention was held in the hall in February, 1886, and 345 teachers were permitted to sit under the instruction of some of the foremost educators of the United States. The teachers continued to gather here each year until 1890, when the plan was adopted to change the meeting place annually.

At this Chautauqua building in 1887 gathered delegates from the coast cities of the South in response to the call of the Coast Defense Association, and adopted a memorial to Congress asking for southern fortifications, arsenals and navy yard.

By 1900 there were over 400 such local assemblies as the one at DeFuniak. In the peak year of 1924 the traveling chautauquas visited 10,000 communities. The decline of the Chautauqua is attributed to movies, radio, automobiles, luncheon clubs and "the greater sophistication of the public." South Florida Chautauquas were operated at Mount Dora and Arcadia.

DOES 'THE COLUMNS' HAVE NICKEL IN EVERY BRICK?

TALLAHASSEE—Tradition has it that a nickel is embedded in every brick of "The Columns," one of the capital city's oldest homes, at N. Adams Street and West Park Avenue. Many who believe this story apparently have probed the bricks near the ground digging for the coins.

Tallahassee editor and historian Malcolm Johnson says there's no foundation for the story, that it stemmed from a remark by the builder that each brick was worth a nickel, that is it cost that much.

The mansion, of Greek Revival architecture, was erected in 1835 by a contractor named Benjamin Chaires from North Carolina. History is not clear on just who was the original owner—one report says it was for a millionaire known as "Money" Williams.

The brick is red, the roof is pitched and four handsome columns are at the entrance. Vine-covered chimneys rise flush with the gable ends.

A Dominican mahogany rail runs along the stairway to the second floor. It's said that the stairs haven't always been in their present position. One of the owners reportedly had the stairs run down through his bedroom on the lower floor. He had an attractive daughter and he feared she might elope with someone who loved her only for her money!

"The Columns" have served many purposes. During the Indian wars, it was used as a refuge from the red man. The first chartered bank in Florida at one time occupied a wing of the house. In modern times, a very popular inn operated here. At present the mansion is owned by the First Baptist Church and is used for a recreation center.

HOME OWNED BY GOVERNOR PERRY STILL STANDS

PENSACOLA—Overlooking downtown Pensacola from a commanding spot on the hill at Palifox Street and Wright Avenue is the Scottish Rite Temple which was the attractive residence of Florida Gov. Edward A. Perry.

History of the building goes back to 1867 when Charles F. Boysen acquired the property and constructed the building which still stands. At one time it sported a cupola. The mansion later served as Consulate of Sweden and Norway.

Mrs. Wathen V. Perry, wife of the Governor, bought the place in 1882, which was shortly before Perry became State Chief Executive. He served from 1885-89. Scottish Rite acquired the property and home in 1922.

Governor Perry, a native of Massachusetts, was graduated from Yale, taught school awhile in Alabama and moved to Pensacola, where he began practicing law in 1856.

The future governor went to war with the Pensacola Rifle Rangers, a volunteer company. He later commanded the Florida Brigade under Gen. Robert E. Lee and served with great distinction in the battles of Fredericksburg and Chancellorsville. Twice wounded, he was discharged as a Brigadier General.

The Florida Constitution of 1885, under which the state functioned until 1969, was drafted at a convention shortly after Perry took office. The administration is noted for establishing the State Board of Education to advance public schools. Governor Perry returned to Pensacola after his term, and died there on October 15, 1889.